SMALL BUSINESS GROWTH BLUEPRINT

A Step-by-Step Plan to Starting and Scaling Your Business

Amy D. Miller

Table of contents

Chapter 1

Introduction.
i. Overview of the importance of growing a small business profitably.

Establishing a small company is a huge accomplishment, but developing it financially is much more vital. Although many entrepreneurs may be pleased with merely keeping their company afloat, the true struggle is in developing the firm and making it profitable. Profitability is a fundamental aspect of every company's development, regardless of its size or sector. Here's an outline of the necessity of developing a small company successfully.

Financial Stability
One of the most important advantages of developing a small company effectively is financial security. When a firm is successful, it has enough cash to meet its expenditures and invest in its development. This implies that the firm can pay its obligations on time, maintain a strong cash flow, and avoid taking on debt. Financial stability is also vital when it comes to

recruiting investors, getting loans, and expanding into new markets.

Market Share

Another key part of running a small firm successfully is expanding market share. When a firm grows, it acquires a greater portion of the market, which may result in more sales and income. By concentrating on profitability, a small firm may reinvest its earnings into marketing, product development, and customer service, all of which can help it gain a greater share of the market.

Employee Satisfaction

Profitability also plays a factor in employee happiness. When a firm is prosperous, it can afford to pay its workers well, give benefits, and provide training and development opportunities. This, in turn, may lead to increased employee satisfaction, fewer turnover rates, and more productive staff.

Innovation

Successful firms have the resources to invest in innovation and create new goods and services. By doing so, businesses may stay ahead of the competition and remain relevant in a continuously changing industry. Innovation may also help small firms separate themselves from their competition and build a distinctive selling proposition that sets them apart.

Community Impact
Lastly, developing a small company successfully may have a good influence on the community. Successful firms can afford to give to philanthropic organizations, sponsor local events, and generate employment. They may also supply goods and services that match the requirements of the community, which can lead to greater consumer loyalty and favorable word-of-mouth.

Developing a small firm financially is vital for its long-term success. It gives financial stability, improves market share, promotes employee happiness, fosters innovation, and has a good influence on the community. By concentrating on profitability, small company owners may develop a sustainable and profitable firm that benefits everyone involved.

ii. Brief explanation of what it means to grow a small business profitably.

Expanding a small firm is a frequent objective for many entrepreneurs. Yet, it is crucial to not just concentrate on expansion but also on expanding profitably. This involves boosting income and profitability while maintaining a sustainable company strategy. In this post, we will offer a basic explanation of what it means to expand a small company successfully.

First and foremost, successful development demands a good company strategy. A business plan covers the aims and strategies of the organization, including financial estimates, marketing initiatives, and operational plans. This strategy should be periodically updated and amended as the firm develops and changes.

Secondly, it is crucial to concentrate on boosting income while minimizing expenditures. This entails finding areas where the organization may improve revenues, such as by expanding into new markets or raising pricing, while simultaneously lowering unneeded expenditures. For example, a small firm may negotiate better prices with suppliers or move to more cost-effective software solutions.

Another crucial part of a successful expansion is investing in the correct resources. This involves recruiting and training the proper staff, investing in technology, and enhancing operational efficiency. By investing in these resources, a small firm may boost productivity and minimize expenses, leading to higher profitability.

Also, a small firm must concentrate on creating good connections with clients. By delivering exceptional customer service and creating a loyal client base, a small firm may grow its revenue and profitability over the long run. This involves listening to client input, reacting to concerns immediately, and delivering unique solutions to match their requirements.

Finally, it is necessary to analyze and track financial parameters consistently to guarantee a profitable growth. This involves measuring income, costs, profit margins, and return on investment (ROI). By frequently reviewing these indicators, a small company may find areas where it can improve and make data-driven choices to promote profitability.

Developing a small company economically needs a sound business strategy that focuses on generating income while limiting expenditures, investing in the necessary resources, creating great connections with clients, and consistently reviewing financial data. By concentrating on five important areas, a small firm may develop and prosper while maintaining a sustainable and successful business model.

Chapter 2

Assessing Your Current Business Operations.

i. Conducting a SWOT analysis to identify strengths, weaknesses, opportunities, and threats.

Conducting a SWOT analysis is an effective approach for any individual or organization to discover its strengths, weaknesses, opportunities, and threats. This analysis may serve in establishing strategies that may build on strengths, eliminate weaknesses, exploit opportunities, and limit hazards.

SWOT stands for strengths, weaknesses, opportunities, and threats. Strengths and weaknesses are internal aspects that are under the control of the individual or organization, while opportunities and threats are external ones that are beyond their control. SWOT analysis is a simple yet powerful strategy that enables individuals or organizations to discover and assess their existing state and build an effective plan.

The following are the stages to execute a SWOT analysis:

Step 1: Define the purpose and scope of the analysis
The first step in completing a SWOT analysis is to establish the purpose and scope of the investigation. This step involves setting the purpose of the analysis, such as evaluating the strengths and weaknesses of a firm or a person, assessing a new product or service, or studying the competitive landscape of a market. The scope of the research should also be specified, including the specific business unit, product line, or market area to be analyzed.

Step 2: Identify strengths
The second step is to discover the strengths of the individual or company. Strengths are the innate attributes that contribute to the success of a person or organization. Some examples of strengths may be a strong brand image, competent employees, an efficient production process, a devoted customer base, or access to unique resources or technology.

Step 3: Identify weaknesses
The third step is to identify the weaknesses of the individual or organization. Weaknesses are the internal concerns that limit the success of an individual or organization. Some examples of disadvantages can include a terrible brand image, a lack of competent labor, an inefficient production process, high employee turnover, or a lack of access to distinctive resources or technologies.

Step 4: Identify opportunities
The fourth step is to identify the opportunities open to the individual or organization. Opportunities are external situations that may be utilized to boost the performance of a person or company. Some examples of opportunities may be a burgeoning market sector, new technology or goods, a favorable regulatory environment, or new alliances or collaborations.

Step 5: Identify hazards
The fifth and final step is to identify the threats presented by the individual or organization. Threats are external elements that could harm the success of a person or organization. Some instances of hazards can include severe

competitiveness, economic downturns, changing client preferences, legislative changes, or natural disasters.

When the SWOT analysis is complete, the next step is to design a strategy that exploits the strengths, minimizes the weaknesses, capitalizes on the opportunities, and mitigates the threats. The strategy should be realistic, actionable, and aligned with the objectives of the individual or organization.

Conducting a SWOT analysis is an important strategy to analyze the present state of a person or business and design an effective plan. By examining strengths, weaknesses, opportunities, and threats, individuals or organizations may build a realistic and executable strategy that may increase their success.

ii. Evaluating financial statements and identifying areas for improvement.

Financial statements offer helpful information about a company's financial position and are crucial for making intelligent decisions. Examining financial records may help find opportunities for improvement and enhance decision-making. In this article, we will study how to evaluate financial records and uncover areas for improvement.

The first stage in reviewing financial statements is to analyze the balance sheet. The balance sheet presents a snapshot of a company's financial situation at a specific point in time. It lists the company's assets, liabilities, and equity. By studying the balance sheet, we may detect trends and changes in a company's financial situation. For example, an increase in liabilities can imply that a corporation is taking on too much debt, while a decline in assets might indicate that a company is not investing in its future growth.

The next step is to assess the income statement. The income statement presents a summary of a company's sales, expenses, and profits within a specific period. By studying the income statement, we may detect trends and changes in a company's revenue and expenditure. For example, if a firm's revenue is declining but expenditures are expanding, it may indicate that the business is not regulating its expenses correctly.

The cash flow statement is another key financial statement that should be evaluated. The cash flow statement depicts the inflows and outflows of cash during a given time. By reviewing the cash flow statement, we may discover the sources and uses of cash and estimate a company's liquidity. For example, if a firm has negative cash flow from operations, it may signal that the company is not making enough cash from its primary activities to cover its expenses.

After examining the financial statements, it is necessary to identify areas for improvement. Some aspects that may deserve improvement include:

Debt management - If a corporation has too much debt, it may be difficult for the company to manage its cash flow and meet its financial responsibilities. In this situation, the firm may need to establish a plan to lower its debt levels.

Cost management - If a company's expenditures are too high, it may be essential to pursue cost-cutting techniques to boost profitability.

Revenue growth - If a company's revenue is declining, it may be necessary to generate new items or services or explore new markets to boost growth.

Working capital management - If a company's working capital is not managed appropriately, it may struggle to meet its short-term financial obligations. In this case, the corporation may need to increase its inventory management or lower its accounts receivable collection time.

Studying financial records is an essential component of conducting a corporation. By reviewing the balance sheet, income statement, and cash flow statement, we may detect trends and changes in a company's financial situation. By identifying areas for improvement, we may build a plan to overcome any financial challenges and raise profitability.

iii. Analyzing market trends and competition.

In today's fast-paced business environment, organizations need to evaluate market trends and competition to remain ahead of the game. Studying market trends and competition gives insights into what consumers want, what rivals are doing, and what the market wants. In this post, we'll cover why market trend analysis and competition analysis are vital for firms and how to do them efficiently.

Why examine market trends and competition?

Studying market trends and competition offers organizations useful information that may help them make educated choices about their marketing and sales strategy. These are some of the primary advantages of studying market trends and competition:

Appreciate consumer requirements and desires
By monitoring market trends, firms may acquire insights into client wants and preferences. This information may help organizations build goods and services that match client requests and expectations.

Identify opportunities and risks

Studying market trends and competition may help organizations discover opportunities and dangers in the industry. This information may be utilized to design plans that take advantage of opportunities and avoid risks.

Keep ahead of the competition

By evaluating competition, organizations may acquire insights into what their rivals are doing and how they are positioning themselves in the market. This information may be utilized to design strategies that distinguish their goods and services and keep them ahead of the competition.

Enhance decision-making

By researching market trends and competition, firms may make better-informed judgments regarding their marketing and sales strategy. This information may help organizations manage resources more efficiently and make better choices regarding pricing, product development, and marketing.

Following are the steps to do a market trend analysis:

Define the market
The first stage in market trend analysis is to define the market. This comprises determining the target audience, geographic area, and industry.

Collect data
The next stage is to gather data on market trends. This may be done via market research, questionnaires, and focus groups. Data may also be acquired via industry reports, news articles, and internet sites.

Analyze the data
After the data is acquired, it has to be examined. This entails recognizing patterns and trends in the data and developing conclusions from the study.

Draw conclusions
The last phase in market trend analysis is to derive conclusions from the study. This entails formulating forecasts about future market trends and designing tactics to take advantage of these trends.

How to perform the competitive analysis?

Following are the steps to perform competitiveness analysis:

Identify competitors
The first stage in competition analysis is to identify the competitors. This entails investigating firms that provide comparable goods or services.

Collect data
The next stage is to acquire data about rivals. This may be done by internet research, reviewing rival websites, and monitoring social media and industry news.

Analyze the data
After the data is acquired, it has to be examined. This entails analyzing the strengths and weaknesses of rivals and how they are positioning themselves in the market.

Develop strategies
The last phase in competition analysis is to establish tactics that distinguish your goods or services from your rivals. This might entail generating distinctive selling propositions,

enhancing product quality or customer service, and optimizing pricing and distribution tactics.

Understanding market trends and competition is vital for firms to remain ahead of the game. By understanding client wants and preferences, finding opportunities and risks, keeping ahead of the competition, and enhancing decision-making, organizations may design successful marketing and sales strategies that promote growth and success.

Chapter 3

Creating a Growth Strategy.
i. Setting realistic goals and objectives.

Establishing realistic goals and objectives is vital for achieving success in every aspect of life. Whether you're pursuing personal or professional objectives, the process of goal-setting takes thorough study and preparation to ensure that your aims are feasible, quantifiable, and meaningful. In this post, we'll discuss several methods for defining realistic goals and objectives that will help you accomplish your intended results.

Determine your priorities and values
Before you start defining objectives, it's necessary to determine your priorities and values. What is most important to you in life? What do you wish to achieve? Knowing your objectives and values can allow you to develop meaningful goals that connect with your overall vision for your life.

Be specific and measurable

While defining objectives, it's crucial to be explicit and quantifiable. Vague objectives like "get in shape" or "save more money" are difficult to fulfill because they lack definition and detail. Instead, define clear objectives that are quantifiable and doable. For example, instead of stating "get in shape," create a goal of "reduce 10 pounds in three months" or "run a 5K in six months."

Establish attainable goals

Although it's vital to aspire high when creating objectives, it's equally necessary to be practical and create reasonable targets. Setting objectives that are too demanding or unreasonable might lead to dissatisfaction and demotivation. Instead, make objectives that are tough yet doable. Divide major objectives down into smaller, more doable stages, and celebrate your success along the way.

Create a plan

After you've established your priorities, values, and clear, realistic objectives, it's time to build a strategy for accomplishing them. Break down your objectives into smaller tasks or milestones and develop a timeframe for achieving each one.

Determine any resources you'll need, such as time, money, or help from others. Having a strategy in place can help you stay focused and motivated and make it easy to measure your progress.

Be flexible

Although it's necessary to have a strategy in place, it's equally important to be flexible and adjust to changing situations. Life is unpredictable, and occasionally unforeseen occurrences or setbacks may ruin even the best-laid plans. Whether you meet barriers or problems along the path, don't give up. Instead, alter your approach as required and remain dedicated to your objectives.

Celebrate your triumphs

Lastly, make sure to appreciate your victories along the way. Establishing and accomplishing goals requires time and work, and it's crucial to appreciate your progress and triumphs. Celebrating your victories will help you remain inspired and devoted to your objectives, and give you the confidence to take on even larger challenges in the future.

Establishing realistic goals and objectives is a vital aspect of achieving success in any area of life. By establishing your objectives and values, making clear and realistic goals, developing a strategy, being adaptable, and celebrating your victories, you may remain focused and motivated as you work toward your intended results. Remember, setting goals is a process, not a one-time event, so be patient, persistent, and devoted to your vision for your life.

ii. Developing a marketing plan.

Creating a marketing strategy is vital for every organization to flourish. A marketing plan is a detailed document that details a company's entire marketing strategy and techniques. It specifies the target audience, establishes marketing objectives, identifies the competitors, and develops a strategy to fulfill the company's goals.

Developing a marketing strategy needs meticulous preparation and research. The following stages will help you establish an efficient marketing strategy for your business:

Determine your target audience:
The first step in building a marketing strategy is to determine your target demographic. Who are your ideal customers? What are their requirements and preferences? By answering these questions, you may personalize your marketing efforts to target your ideal clients.

Doing market research: Market research is vital for establishing an effective marketing strategy. It may assist you in detecting market trends, client preferences, and competitors. Research may be undertaken using questionnaires, focus groups, and Internet research tools.

Establish marketing goals. The next stage is to identify your marketing objectives. What do you hope to accomplish with your marketing efforts? Your goals should be explicit, quantifiable, attainable, relevant, and time-bound.

Create a marketing plan: Once you have defined your target audience, completed market research, and established marketing goals, you can build a marketing strategy. Your plan should define how you will contact your target audience, market your goods or services, and separate yourself from the competition.

Decide on your budget. Your marketing budget will define the breadth of your marketing activities. You need to evaluate how much money you are willing to spend on marketing and allocate resources appropriately.

Identify your techniques: Your marketing methods should be linked to your marketing strategy and goals. Your techniques might include social media marketing, email marketing, advertising, events, or public relations.

Assess and adapt: Finally, it's crucial to evaluate the efficacy of your marketing campaign and change your approaches accordingly. You may use tools like Google Analytics to measure your website traffic and social media analytics to track your social media success.

Creating a marketing strategy is a key component of every successful organization. By identifying your target audience, performing market research, creating marketing goals, building a marketing strategy, calculating your budget, defining your methods, and monitoring and changing your plan, you can construct an effective marketing plan that promotes company success.

iii. Identifying growth opportunities.

Finding growth opportunities is a vital component of company strategy that helps organizations develop and remain competitive. In today's continuously changing and highly competitive industry, organizations must always explore new methods to develop and improve. By recognizing growth possibilities, firms may design and execute plans to capitalize on those chances and achieve sustainable development.

These are some essential actions that firms may take to find growth opportunities:

Evaluate market trends and consumer demands
To find growth prospects, organizations must first assess market trends and client demands. This entails examining market trends, assessing customer behavior, and knowing the competitors. Companies must identify the unmet wants and aspirations of their consumers, as well as the holes in the market that their goods or services may fill.

Emphasis on innovation
Innovation is a crucial engine of growth in today's economy. By concentrating on

innovation, organizations may create new goods, services, and processes that can help them acquire a competitive advantage. This may entail investing in research and development, working with other firms or organizations, or investigating new technologies.

Discover new markets

Another strategy to uncover growth prospects is to investigate new markets. Expansion may entail expanding into new geographic areas, targeting new client categories, or building new distribution methods. By extending their reach, firms may improve their income streams and tap into new avenues of growth.

Create a culture of constant improvement

Lastly, firms must cultivate a culture of continuous improvement to find and capitalize on growth prospects. This means fostering innovation, investing in personnel training and development, and regularly analyzing and refining corporate procedures. By continually improving, organizations may remain ahead of the curve and uncover new chances for development.

Finding growth possibilities is a vital component of corporate strategy. By evaluating market trends and consumer demands, doing a SWOT analysis, concentrating on innovation, exploring new markets, and establishing a culture of continuous improvement, organizations may discover potential areas for development and build plans to capitalize on those possibilities. By doing so, they may achieve sustainable development and remain competitive in today's changing business market.

iv. Developing a plan for financing growth.

As a company owner, you may want to grow your firm and generate income. But, funding development may be a hard undertaking, particularly if you don't have a strategy in place. Having a strategy for funding growth is vital to guaranteeing that you have adequate resources to execute your expansion goals effectively.

These are some stages to establishing a strategy for funding growth:

Evaluate your present financial condition: The first step in building a strategy for funding expansion is to examine your current financial situation. Evaluate your cash flow, income sources, and costs to estimate how much money you have available for expansion.

Determine your growth goals: Define your development objectives and the resources required to attain them. These objectives might be short-term or long-term and can involve growing your product range, accessing new markets, or boosting manufacturing capacity.

Investigate finance possibilities: After you have determined your growth objectives and the resources required, research financing solutions that correspond with your company's requirements. Other financing alternatives include bank loans, venture capital, crowdsourcing, and angel investors.

Assess the benefits and downsides of each funding option: Each financing option has its merits and downsides. Assess the risks and rewards of each option before making a choice. Evaluate considerations such as interest rates, payback periods, and the extent of control you are ready to give up.

Create a finance plan: Establish a financing strategy that corresponds with your growth objectives and financial status. Your approach should contain the funding possibilities you have identified, the quantity of money you need, and the schedule for getting the cash.

Develop a financial plan: Develop a financial strategy that details your income predictions, costs, and cash flow. This strategy should also contain a budget for funding expansion and a payback schedule for any loans or investments.

Track your progress: After you have devised a strategy for funding expansion, it is crucial to review your progress periodically. Evaluate your financial accounts and revise your strategy as required to ensure that you are on pace to meet your development objectives.

Having a strategy for funding development is vital for the success of your organization. By assessing your current financial situation, identifying your growth goals, exploring financing options, evaluating the pros and cons of each option, developing a financing strategy, creating a financial plan, and monitoring your progress, you can ensure that you have enough resources to execute your expansion plans successfully. Remember to contact financial experts and specialists before making any important financial choices.

Chapter 4

Improving Operational Efficiency.
i. Streamlining processes and procedures.

In today's fast-paced world, organizations are continuously seeking methods to enhance efficiency, cut expenses, and boost production. One of the most efficient methods to attain these objectives is through simplifying processes and procedures. Streamlining refers to the act of simplifying and refining current processes to make them more effective, whereas procedures refer to the set of steps that personnel take to execute a certain job.

Streamlining processes and procedures includes a detailed examination of all the activities involved in a certain process. It entails finding inefficiencies and bottlenecks in the process, removing superfluous stages, and optimizing the remaining phases to ensure they are done as effectively as possible. This might entail restructuring activities, removing redundancies, and automating key stages.

One of the most important advantages of simplifying processes and procedures is that it may lead to considerable cost reductions. By removing inefficiencies and redundancies, firms may minimize the amount of time and resources necessary to execute a job, resulting in reduced costs and increased profitability. In addition, simplifying may also lower the likelihood of errors and mistakes, which can save even more money by avoiding expensive rework or repairs.

Another key advantage of simplifying processes and procedures is that it may enhance productivity and staff morale. When workers are working with effective, streamlined procedures, they may finish their tasks more quickly and with less aggravation. This may lead to better work satisfaction, less stress, and enhanced overall productivity.

To simplify processes and procedures, firms should start by sketching out the whole process and identifying each step involved. This may be done using flowcharts, diagrams, or other visual tools. After the process is drawn out, it's necessary to identify areas of inefficiency or duplication and discover strategies to simplify or remove those stages. This can entail integrating new technology or automation, rearranging work, or altering the way personnel is taught.

It's also crucial to regularly examine and monitor the efficiency of any simplifying initiatives. This might entail collecting and evaluating data on the process's efficiency, finding any new bottlenecks or inefficiencies, and making improvements as appropriate. By regularly monitoring and adjusting processes and procedures, firms can guarantee they are always functioning at optimal efficiency.

Streamlining processes and procedures is a vital part of enhancing productivity and decreasing expenses in any firm. By finding inefficiencies and streamlining current processes, firms may enhance productivity, minimize mistakes, and boost profitability. With a full evaluation of procedures and continuous monitoring and improvement efforts, firms may achieve continued success in simplifying their operations.

ii. Implementing technology solutions.

Adopting technological solutions is a vital step that firms must undertake to boost productivity, efficiency, and competitiveness. Nonetheless, the procedure may be complex and daunting, particularly for firms that lack technical skills or experience. Effective technology deployment involves careful planning, stakeholder buy-in, and a clear grasp of the organization's objectives and goals. In this post, we will explore the important procedures and considerations for integrating technological solutions into enterprises.

Step 1: Determine the Problem or Opportunity

The first step in deploying technological solutions is to identify the issue or opportunity that the company is aiming to solve. This might be anything from cutting expenses to boosting customer service to enhancing productivity. After the issue or opportunity has been recognized, it is vital to clearly define the scope of the project, including the goals, objectives, and intended results.

Step 2: Perform a Needs Assessment

Before deploying any technological solution, it is vital to undertake a needs assessment to establish the particular requirements of the company. This comprises examining the present processes, systems, and workflows, identifying the gaps and inefficiencies, and outlining the main features and functions necessary for the new solution.

Step 3: Research and Pick a Technological Solution

Based on the needs assessment, the next stage is to study and pick a technological solution that corresponds with the organization's objectives and goals. This involves analyzing multiple possibilities, such as off-the-shelf software, bespoke software development, or cloud-based solutions, and comparing features, cost, and support options. It is crucial to include key stakeholders in the selection process to guarantee buy-in and alignment with the organization's overall strategy.

Step 4: Create an Implementation Plan

After a technological solution has been chosen, the next step is to establish an implementation strategy that describes the main actions, dates, and resources necessary to properly install the system. This involves defining the roles and responsibilities of the project team, building a communication strategy, identifying possible risks and mitigation techniques, and implementing a training plan to ensure that end-users are comfortable with the new system.

Step 5: Test and Deploy the Solution

Before implementing the technological solution, it is vital to do extensive testing to confirm that the system is running effectively and satisfies the organization's needs. This involves testing for functionality, usability, performance, and security. After testing is complete, the solution may be implemented in a staged manner, beginning with a small group of users and progressively spreading to the entire business.

Step 6: Monitor and Assess the Solution

When the technological solution has been installed, it is vital to monitor and analyze its performance to verify that it is fulfilling the organization's goals and objectives. This involves monitoring key performance metrics, such as adoption rates, user happiness, and productivity, and making modifications as required to maximize the system's performance.

Deploying technological solutions may be a complicated and demanding process, but with careful planning, stakeholder buy-in, and a clear knowledge of the company's objectives and goals, it can be a profitable investment in the future success of the business. By following the main stages and considerations indicated in this article, companies may effectively adopt technological solutions that boost productivity, efficiency, and competitiveness.

iii. Optimizing staffing and team management.

Optimizing staffing and team management may be a hard endeavor, but there are various methods you can employ to make the process more productive. Here are some tips:

Evaluate your present team: Before making any changes, take a good look at your current team. Identify strengths, weaknesses, and skill gaps. This can assist you in evaluating what modifications need to be made to maximize your personnel.

Establish duties and responsibilities: Clearly describe the tasks and responsibilities of each team member. This will help ensure that everyone understands what is expected of them and decrease the risk of overlapping work.

Evaluate workload: Determine whether any team members are overworked or underused. Modify the workload as required to ensure that each team member is working at their potential without burning out.

Promote cross-training: Encourage team members to gain new talents and cross-train in other areas. This helps to establish a more flexible and adaptive team and may be advantageous during peak seasons or when particular team members are away.

Consider outsourcing: Consider outsourcing specific jobs or projects to freelancers or contractors. This may be a cost-effective alternative and enable your staff to concentrate on vital duties.

Promote open communication: Support open communication amongst team members. This may assist in managing disagreements, detecting issues early on, and establishing a healthy work atmosphere.

Monitor performance: Periodically monitor team performance to ensure that everyone is meeting expectations. Give comments and assistance as required to help team members develop.

By applying these tactics, you may optimize your staffing and team management, which will eventually lead to increased productivity, higher work satisfaction, and superior business results.

iv. Improving customer service.

Customer service is a key part of every organization. It is the image that a business portrays to the public and may create or ruin the reputation of the firm. Delivering exceptional customer service may lead to better client satisfaction, repeat business, and, eventually, more profitability. On the other side, bad customer service may lead to unfavorable evaluations, client attrition, and lost money. In this post, we will cover various methods that organizations may use to enhance their customer service.

Train personnel correctly: One of the most significant strategies to enhance customer service is to ensure that employees are properly taught. They should be informed about the items or services they are offering and able to answer any queries that clients may have. Also, they should be instructed on how to deal with tough clients and how to manage complaints properly.

Establish a customer-centric culture: To deliver exceptional customer service, it is vital to building a customer-centric culture inside the firm. This implies that all staff should be focused on putting the client first and ensuring that their requirements are addressed. This may be done by creating customer service objectives, giving rewards for exceptional customer service, and rewarding workers that go above and beyond in their customer service efforts.

Utilize technology to enhance customer service: technology may be used to improve customer service in a variety of ways. For example, companies may utilize chatbots to provide 24/7 service to clients. Companies may also utilize social media to communicate with clients and respond to their inquiries and concerns in real time. Moreover, firms may utilize customer relationship management (CRM) software to keep track of client interactions and deliver tailored service.

Customize customer service: Customers like individualized treatment. Companies may utilize data and analytics to obtain information about their customers' tastes and buying histories and use this information to create personalized suggestions and offers. Also, companies may leverage the customer's name and other personal information to make them feel valued and appreciated.

React to customer complaints promptly: No matter how fantastic a company's customer service is, there will always be occasions when a client is unsatisfied. When this occurs, it is crucial to react to the complaint swiftly and efficiently. This entails listening to the customer's problems, apologizing for any trouble caused, and giving a solution to the situation.

Enhancing customer service is vital for every organization that wants to flourish. By educating people correctly, building a customer-centric culture, leveraging technology to enhance service, customizing customer care, and reacting to complaints immediately, companies may deliver exceptional customer service and create a loyal client base. By doing so, businesses will not only boost client happiness but also increase their profitability.

Chapter 5

Expanding Your Market Reach.
i. Identifying new customer segments.

Finding new consumer groups is a critical component of any company strategy. By knowing the requirements and preferences of distinct consumer groups, organizations may customize their goods, services, and marketing activities to successfully reach and engage these segments. In this article, we will cover some of the important procedures involved in finding new client segments and explain why organizations must undergo this process.

Conduct market research
The first stage in discovering new client categories is to undertake detailed market research. This entails gathering data on consumer behavior, preferences, and requirements via surveys, focus groups, and other market research approaches. The information obtained should be examined to detect patterns and trends in consumer behavior and preferences. This data may assist firms in identifying the characteristics and desires of

distinct client categories, such as age, gender, economic level, geographic region, and lifestyle.

Examine customer data

The next stage is to assess the client data that the organization already has on hand. This may include sales statistics, customer feedback, and other consumer information obtained via multiple means. By evaluating this data, organizations may acquire insights into the purchasing behaviors, tastes, and requirements of various client categories. This information may be utilized to construct targeted marketing campaigns and modify goods and services to fit the individual demands of each consumer group.

Segment the customer base

After the market research and customer data analysis are complete, the next step is to segment the customer base. This entails dividing clients with comparable qualities and wants into discrete segments. These divisions may be based on demographics, psychographics, or other variables that are important to the company. For example, a clothes store may segment its clients depending on age, gender, and style choice.

Build personalities

After segmenting the client base, organizations should construct personas for each consumer segment. These personas are imaginary characters who reflect the average client in each area. They are built based on the data obtained during market research and consumer data analysis. Personas help organizations better understand the requirements, preferences, and behaviors of each consumer group, which may guide product development and marketing activities.

Test and refine

After the personas are formed, firms should test and modify them via consumer feedback and data analysis. This ensures that the personas reflect the requirements and interests of each consumer category. By regularly testing and refining the personas, organizations can guarantee that their goods, services, and marketing activities are matched with the requirements and preferences of each client group.

Finding new consumer groups is a vital component of any company strategy. By knowing the requirements and preferences of distinct consumer groups, organizations may customize their goods, services, and marketing activities to successfully reach and engage these segments. The process of finding new client segments comprises performing market research, evaluating customer data, segmenting the consumer base, building personas, and testing and refining. By following these procedures, organizations may obtain a better knowledge of their consumers and enhance their overall performance.

ii. Developing new products or services.

Creating new goods or services is a crucial component of corporate development and survival. The process of bringing a new product or service to market may be tough and time-consuming, but with the correct strategy, it can also be satisfying and lucrative. In this post, we will discuss the phases involved in creating new goods or services, from concept genesis through launch.

Idea Generation
The first stage in establishing a new product or service is to create ideas. This may be done via brainstorming meetings, market research, consumer feedback, and industry trends. The idea is to find a need or gap in the market that your product or service can address.

Concept Development
After you have an idea, you need to build a concept for your product or service. This requires producing a clear and succinct explanation of what your product or service is, what issue it answers, and how it will benefit consumers. It is also crucial to define your target

market and understand its demands and preferences.

Feasibility Analysis

Before investing time and money into creating your product or service, it is vital to undertake a feasibility study. This entails examining the technical, financial, and commercial viability of your proposal. You may need to undertake market research, construct a prototype, and evaluate expenses and possible income.

Product/Service Development

After you have concluded that your concept is realistic, you may begin constructing your product or service. This entails generating a thorough strategy and timeframe, designing and testing prototypes, and improving your idea based on input from consumers and stakeholders.

Testing and Validation

Before introducing your product or service, it is vital to test and verify it. This might entail running focus groups, beta testing with a restricted set of clients, and collecting input from industry experts. The purpose is to discover any difficulties or concerns and make any required improvements before launching.

Launch

After you have tested and confirmed your product or service, it is time to launch it. This comprises devising a marketing plan, preparing promotional materials, and exposing your product or service to your target market. It is crucial to monitor sales and consumer feedback and make any required modifications to guarantee the success of your launch.

Post-Launch Evaluation

After introducing your product or service, it is crucial to assess its success. Monitoring entails monitoring sales, consumer feedback, and market trends. You may need to make improvements to your product or service or marketing approach based on this input to guarantee continuous success.

Creating new goods or services is a crucial component of corporate development and survival. The process encompasses generating ideas, creating a concept, completing a feasibility study, building your product or service, testing and validating, launching, and conducting a post-launch review. By following these steps, you may boost your chances of success and produce goods or services that fit the demands and preferences of your target market.

iii. Expanding geographically.

Expansion geographically may be an exciting opportunity for organizations trying to develop and access new customers. But it is not without its obstacles. From managing cultural differences to dealing with logistics, there are numerous issues to consider when expanding into a new place. In this post, we will cover some of the major aspects that firms should bear in mind while growing regionally.

Market Research and Analysis

When expanding into a new market, it is vital to perform extensive study and analysis. This involves acquiring data on the local economy, customer behavior, and competition in the target market. It is also necessary to identify any legal and regulatory obligations that may influence the firm.

By performing market research and analysis, companies may acquire a better knowledge of the potential demand for their goods or services, and identify any particular problems that they may have when entering the new market. This information may allow organizations to design a thorough market entry plan that takes into consideration the local market dynamics and establishes realistic objectives and ambitions.

Cultural Differences

While expanding globally, firms must also consider the cultural distinctions between their home market and the target market. This comprises language, conventions, traditions, and values. Failing to appreciate and accept these cultural variations may result in misunderstandings, insults, and even failure.

To prevent these challenges, firms should engage in cross-cultural training and education for their staff, and cooperate with local partners and consultants who have a strong grasp of the target market's culture. This will assist firms in changing their goods, services, and marketing methods to better fit the demands and preferences of the local market.

Logistics and Infrastructure

Expanding geographically also includes dealing with logistical and infrastructural difficulties. This encompasses transportation, distribution, and supply chain management. Companies must ensure that they have the appropriate infrastructure and resources in place to efficiently and successfully provide their goods or services to clients in the new market.

This may necessitate working with local logistics providers and distributors that have a thorough grasp of the local market and can provide the required assistance and experience. It may also entail investing in new technology and systems to simplify processes and boost efficiency.

Legal and Regulatory Considerations

Lastly, organizations must also examine the legal and regulatory needs of the target market. This encompasses concerns like taxes, licensing, and intellectual property protection. Failing to comply with local rules and regulations may result in considerable financial and legal consequences, as well as harm to the company's image.

To handle these legal and regulatory problems, firms should cooperate with local consultants and legal specialists who have a strong grasp of the local legal system and regulatory environment. This will allow firms to guarantee compliance with local rules and regulations, and prevent any possible legal concerns that might limit their performance in the new market.

Expansion geographically may be a hard but profitable opportunity for organizations trying to develop and reach new customers. By conducting thorough market research and analysis, understanding cultural differences, dealing with logistics and infrastructure challenges, and navigating legal and regulatory considerations, businesses can develop a comprehensive market entry strategy that sets them up for success in the new market.

iv. Entering new markets or industries.

Joining a new market or business may be a scary job, but it can also be a satisfying and successful one. Whether you're wanting to grow your present company or start a new endeavor, there are certain actions you can take to boost your chances of success.

These are some crucial considerations when entering a new market or industry:

Conduct your research: When entering a new market, it's necessary to undertake an extensive study. This involves identifying the market size, rivals, prospective consumers, and any regulatory or legal requirements. This material will help you evaluate the possible dangers and possibilities of entering a new market.

Create a strategy: After you have a better grasp of the market, you can design a plan for joining it. This can entail establishing a new product or service, modifying a current one, or working with other firms. Your approach should be guided by your research and linked with your company's objectives.

Establish partnerships: Developing ties with prospective consumers, partners, and suppliers is vital when entering a new market. Networking events, conferences, and trade shows may be terrific opportunities to meet new people and develop connections.

Test your assumptions: Before investing extensively in a new market, it's necessary to evaluate your assumptions. This can include executing a pilot program or selling a restricted version of your product or service to a small set of clients. This can help you discover any possible challenges and modify your plan before expanding.

Be adaptable: Entering a new market may be unexpected, so it's crucial to be flexible and open to change. This can mean changing your approach based on fresh knowledge or pivoting to a different market entirely.

Remain concentrated: Although it's necessary to be adaptable, it's equally crucial to stay focused on your objectives. Don't be distracted by every new opportunity that comes your way. Instead, keep focused on your core business and long-term ambitions.

Measure your success: Lastly, it's crucial to assess your success when entering a new market. This could entail measuring indicators like as customer acquisition, revenue, and market share. This can help you evaluate if your plan is working and make changes as required.

Entering a new market or sector may be tough, but with the correct research, plan, and mentality, it can also be a satisfying and successful experience. By following these important factors, you may boost your chances of success and position your firm for development and expansion.

Chapter 6

Managing Your Finances.
i. Budgeting and forecasting.

Budgeting and forecasting are two key activities in corporate planning. They are crucial tools that help organizations prepare for the future and make educated choices based on their financial status. Budgeting and forecasting are closely connected but differ in terms of their emphasis, time range, and degree of information included.

Budgeting is the act of making a plan for how a corporation will spend its financial resources over a given time, often a year. It is a thorough financial plan that describes how much money a firm plans to spend and make within the budget period. Budgets are vital for firms of all sizes because they help regulate expenditure, manage cash flow, and allocate resources properly.

The budgeting process often includes examining historical financial data, identifying possible income sources and costs, creating financial objectives, and allocating resources to meet those goals. The budgeting process is normally completed yearly; however, some firms may develop quarterly or monthly budgets for particular projects or divisions.

On the other hand, forecasting is the practice of predicting future financial results based on past data and other pertinent criteria. It entails examining historical performance, finding patterns, and estimating future revenues and costs. Forecasting is vital because it enables organizations to anticipate and plan for changes in the market and alter their strategy accordingly.

There are two basic forms of forecasting: qualitative and quantitative. Qualitative forecasting is based on expert views and judgment, whereas quantitative forecasting employs statistical models and data analysis to produce predictions. Both methods of forecasting may be utilized in budgeting and are vital for making realistic financial plans.

Budgeting and forecasting are crucial activities for organizations of all sizes. They assist firms to plan for the future, regulate expenditures, manage cash flow, and allocate resources wisely. By generating realistic budgets and projections, firms can make educated choices about where to spend their resources and how to accomplish their financial objectives.

Budgeting and forecasting are crucial tools for organizations to prepare for the future and make educated choices based on their financial status. They are closely similar yet vary in terms of their purpose, period, and amount of detail involved. By doing precise budgeting and forecasting, organizations may manage their money efficiently and accomplish their financial objectives.

ii. Managing cash flow.

Controlling cash flow is a vital component of operating a successful company. Cash flow is the movement of money in and out of a firm, and it is crucial to guarantee that there is always enough cash available to satisfy financial commitments.

There are various methods that firms may employ to manage their cash flow properly. They include predicting, monitoring, and regulating cash flow.

Predicting cash flow includes forecasting the projected inflows and outflows of cash over a certain time. This may be done by studying past financial data, industry trends, and market circumstances. By projecting cash flow, firms may anticipate future financial gaps and take steps to solve them before they become an issue.

Monitoring cash flow includes monitoring actual cash inflows and outflows in real time. This may be done using financial software or spreadsheets. By monitoring cash flow, organizations may rapidly notice any unexpected changes or variations in cash flow and take necessary action to avoid any negative repercussions.

Managing cash flow entails regulating the timing of cash inputs and outflows. This may be done by negotiating advantageous payment terms with suppliers, granting incentives for early payments from consumers, and maintaining inventory levels to minimize overstocking. By regulating cash flow, organizations may guarantee that cash is accessible when it is needed and limit the risk of financial deficits.

Another crucial part of controlling cash flow is having a cash reserve. A cash reserve is a pool of cash that is set aside to meet unforeseen bills or financial deficits. The amount of the cash reserve will depend on the size and type of the firm, but as a general guideline, it should be adequate to cover at least three months of costs.

In addition to these techniques, firms should also explore employing financing solutions to manage cash flow. They may include lines of credit, company loans, or factoring. Nonetheless, it is vital to thoroughly assess the costs and hazards connected with these choices before pursuing them.

Controlling cash flow is vital for the success of any firm. By anticipating, monitoring, and regulating cash flow, companies may guarantee that they have adequate cash available to satisfy financial commitments and prevent cash deficits. However, keeping a cash reserve and researching financing solutions may provide extra security against unexpected spending or cash flow problems.

iii. Seeking financing and funding opportunities.

Whether you are beginning a new company, growing an existing one, or embarking on a new project, pursuing finance and funding alternatives is vital to success. There are several choices accessible to companies and people wishing to get finance, ranging from typical bank loans to venture capital investments. In this post, we will examine some of the numerous financing and funding alternatives available and give information on how to pick the right solution for your requirements.

Conventional Bank Loans
One of the most typical methods to get finance for your company or project is via a regular bank loan. Banks will examine your creditworthiness and ask for security in return for a loan. These loans are often less hazardous than other forms of financing, and banks will normally give lower interest rates compared to other lenders.

When asking for a bank loan, it's crucial to have a sound business plan in place and to be prepared to offer paperwork to back your financial accounts. This comprises balance sheets, income statements, and cash flow estimates. You should also be prepared to offer collateral, like equipment, property, or accounts receivable, to secure the loan.

Crowdfunding

Crowdfunding has become a popular technique for entrepreneurs seeking finance for their ideas or enterprises. Crowdfunding is the practice of raising money by having a large number of individuals give modest sums of money. There are various venues accessible for crowdsourcing, including Kickstarter and GoFundMe.

To succeed with crowdfunding, you need to have a clear and appealing narrative about your idea or company. You also need to have a strong social media presence and be prepared to commit time and effort to advertise your campaign.

Venture Capital

Venture capital is a sort of finance where investors offer money to startups and small enterprises in return for stock in the firm. Venture capitalists are often seeking firms with great growth potential and are ready to take on a large degree of risk in exchange for a potentially high return on their investment.

To receive venture capital investment, you need to have a good business strategy and be able to show that your organization has the potential for considerable development. You should also be prepared to give up a percentage of your ownership in the firm in return for money.

Angel Investors
Angel investors are people who contribute capital to startups and small enterprises in return for stock in the firm. Angel investors are often more hands-on than venture capitalists and may give mentorship and direction to the firm.

To receive money from an angel investor, you need to have a compelling business plan and be able to show that your firm has the potential for considerable development. You should also be prepared to give up a percentage of your ownership in the firm in return for money.

Grants
Grants are another option for acquiring cash for your company or project. Grants are often granted by government agencies, charities, and other groups to fund certain sorts of projects or efforts. The application procedure for grants may

be time-consuming, and there is typically a lot of competition for funds.

To get a grant, you need to have a comprehensive grasp of the criteria and standards for the grant program. You should also be able to show that your project or company matches the aims of the grant program.

There are different financing and funding possibilities accessible to entrepreneurs and people wishing to get finance for their company or project. Each choice has its pros and cons, and it's crucial to pick the one that best corresponds with your objectives and requirements. By carefully examining your alternatives and being prepared to offer documents and collateral, you may boost your chances of receiving the cash you need to succeed.

iv. Measuring and tracking financial performance.

Monitoring and tracking financial success is critical for every company or organization. It helps you monitor your financial health and make educated choices to enhance your bottom line. In this post, we will explore the necessity of monitoring and tracking financial performance, several techniques for doing so, and how to utilize this data to make strategic choices.

Why measure and monitor financial performance?

Monitoring and tracking financial success is vital for various reasons, including:

Detect Trends: By evaluating your financial performance, you may spot patterns in your organization. For example, you may see that your income has been rising gradually over the past several months while your costs have been relatively steady. This information may help you make educated choices about how to manage your resources and prepare for the future.

Establish Goals: Monitoring financial performance helps you create realistic financial objectives for your firm. For example, you may wish to raise your sales by 10% during the following quarter. By analyzing your financial performance, you can determine if you are on track to accomplish this target or whether you need to change your plan.

Measure Success: Monitoring financial performance is an excellent technique for assessing whether your organization is successful or not. By monitoring important financial variables such as sales, costs, and profit margins, you may assess if your firm is expanding or shrinking.

Various Approaches for Assessing and Tracking Financial Performance

There are various approaches for assessing and monitoring financial success. Some of the more frequent ways include:

Financial Statements: Financial statements, such as income statements, balance sheets, and cash flow statements, are key instruments for assessing and tracking financial performance.

These statements give a complete picture of your business's financial health and help you discover patterns and make educated choices.

Key Performance Indicators (KPIs): KPIs are precise measurements that are used to monitor performance. For example, revenue growth rate, gross profit margin, and return on investment (ROI) are all KPIs that may be used to measure financial success.

Budgeting: Budgeting is a crucial tool for measuring financial success. By developing a budget, you may set financial objectives and track your progress toward attaining them. This might assist you in finding areas where you need to minimize expenses or spend more resources.

Utilizing Financial Performance Data to Create Strategic Decisions

After you have assessed and monitored your financial performance, you may utilize this data to make strategic choices. For example, if you see that your expenditures are greater than your income, you may need to minimize costs to enhance your profitability. Conversely, if you find that your income is expanding continuously, you may wish to spend more resources on marketing and sales to sustain this growth pattern.

Monitoring and tracking financial performance is vital for every company or organization. It helps you monitor your financial health, create objectives, and make educated choices to enhance your bottom line. By employing financial statements, KPIs, and budgeting, you can monitor your financial performance and utilize this data to make strategic choices.

Chapter 7

Scaling Your Business.
i. Building partnerships and collaborations.

In today's fast-paced and competitive corporate environment, developing partnerships and collaborations are important for success. Collaboration allows firms to combine their capabilities, resources, and networks to accomplish shared objectives. Partnerships and collaborations give firms the chance to exploit each other's experience, skills, and knowledge, which can help generate growth, innovation, and profitability.

There are several advantages to forming partnerships and collaborations, including greater market share, enhanced efficiency, decreased costs, and access to new markets and consumers. Collaborations also allow organizations to share risks and overcome obstacles to entry, which may be especially useful for small and medium-sized enterprises (SMEs).

Establishing partnerships and collaborations needs careful strategy and execution. The first stage is to discover suitable partners who share your values, vision, and ambitions. It's crucial to seek partners that match your strengths and shortcomings and whose talents and resources may offer value to your organization.

After you have identified possible partners, it's crucial to create clear communication routes and set clear expectations. This involves defining the scope and goals of the partnership as well as identifying roles, duties, and dates. It's also vital to build strong governance structures and decision-making procedures to guarantee that the partnership operates smoothly and meets its goals.

To develop effective partnerships and collaborations, it's necessary to foster a culture of trust, openness, and open communication. This involves creating good relationships with partners based on mutual respect and understanding, as well as exchanging information and comments freely and honestly. Frequent communication and cooperation are crucial to creating solid relationships and attaining shared objectives.

Another crucial component in developing effective partnerships and collaborations is a commitment to ongoing development. This entails routinely analyzing the collaboration's success, finding areas for improvement, and taking action to address these issues. It's also crucial to be flexible and adaptive since partnerships may change over time and may need tweaks to guarantee their continuous success.

Establishing partnerships and collaborations is vital for firms wanting to achieve growth, innovation, and profitability. By using each other's capabilities and resources, firms may accomplish more substantial achievements than they could on their own. But developing successful partnerships and collaborations involves careful preparation, good communication, and a commitment to ongoing development. By adopting these principles, organizations may develop great relationships that fuel growth, innovation, and success.

ii. Franchising or licensing opportunities.

Franchise and licensing are two common business formats that allow entrepreneurs the option to start a company with a proven idea and an existing brand. These models enable prospective company entrepreneurs to harness the knowledge and resources of existing firms to boost their chances of success.

Franchising includes the licensing of a brand, a system, and support services by the franchisor to the franchisee, who then conducts a company using the franchisor's brand and system. The franchisor offers training, marketing support, and continuing assistance to help the franchisee operate a successful company. In return, the franchisee pays an initial franchise fee and periodic royalties to the franchisor.

Licensing, on the other hand, entails the licensing of rights to use a brand, product, or service to another party in return for a price or royalty. The licensor maintains ownership over the brand and the product or service, while the licensee is responsible for producing, marketing, and distributing the licensed product or service.

Both franchising and licensing have their pros and cons, and aspiring company owners must understand which model is best suited for their objectives and resources.

One of the key benefits of franchising is the opportunity to use an existing brand and business framework. Franchisees benefit from the franchisor's expertise and knowledge, as well as their marketing and advertising efforts, which may help them grow a client base more rapidly. Moreover, franchisors generally give continuous training and assistance to help franchisees operate their companies efficiently.

Another benefit of franchising is the decreased risk involved compared to establishing a company from scratch. Franchisees get access to an established business model, which decreases the probability of failure. Franchisees can benefit from the franchisor's existing contacts with suppliers and vendors, which may result in cheaper prices for supplies and equipment.

Yet, franchising also has its downsides. The initial franchise cost and annual royalties might be high, which can be a barrier to entry for certain businesses. Franchisees are also forced to follow the franchisor's established system, which might restrict their capacity to make autonomous choices and modifications to the firm.

Licensing, on the other hand, gives entrepreneurs the option to profit from an established brand and product or service without the considerable expenditures involved with franchising. Licensing also gives additional freedom, since licensees have more control over the product or service and may make adjustments and alterations to fit their market.

Yet, licensing also has its downsides. Licensees are responsible for all parts of the company, including production, marketing, and distribution, which may be tough for entrepreneurs without expertise in these areas. However, licensees have less help and supervision from the licensor compared to franchisees, which might make it more difficult to succeed.

Franchising and licensing offer aspiring business owners the opportunity to start a business with an established brand and system. Each model has its advantages and disadvantages, and entrepreneurs should carefully consider their goals and resources before choosing a model. Those who prioritize brand recognition and support may be better suited for franchising, while those who value flexibility and independence may be better suited for licensing. Regardless of the chosen model, entrepreneurs need to conduct thorough research and seek professional advice before making a decision.

iii. Mergers and acquisitions.

Mergers and acquisitions (M&A) refer to the process of integrating two or more enterprises into a single organization. M&A has become a vital strategy for organizations wanting to develop and extend their market share. It encompasses different factors such as due diligence, appraisal, negotiation, and integration.

M&A may take numerous forms, such as horizontal mergers, vertical mergers, conglomerate mergers, and acquisitions. In a horizontal merger, two firms in the same industry of comparable size join forces to increase market share and eliminate rivalry. A "vertical merger" is when a business buys another in the same industry but at a different level of the value chain. A conglomerate merger combines two or more firms that are unconnected in terms of industry and product lines.

Acquisitions, on the other hand, entail one firm purchasing another. The acquiring business may obtain control over the acquired company via numerous tactics, such as a hostile takeover, a friendly takeover, or a leveraged buyout.

M&A may help firms in numerous ways. Firstly, it helps enterprises extend their market share, therefore boosting revenue and profits. M&A may also assist corporations to minimize competition, especially in the case of horizontal mergers. Secondly, it helps organizations diversify their product lines and business operations, decreasing dependence on a particular product or market. Finally, it may assist organizations to obtain new technology or intellectual property, leading to innovation and new product creation. Thirdly, M&A may assist organizations to realize cost reductions via economies of scale and pooled resources.

Yet, M&A may also be hazardous and may not always lead to the intended consequences. It may be tough to combine two diverse business cultures and management styles, resulting in conflict and a loss of productivity. There may also be pushback from workers and stakeholders of the acquired firm, resulting in a drop in morale and performance. Additionally, M&A may be pricey, with transaction fees, legal expenses, and integration costs piling up.

Effective M&A needs rigorous strategy, analysis, and execution. Due diligence is required to discover possible risks and advantages of the acquisition. Valuation is crucial to verify that the transaction is fair and reasonable. Negotiation entails agreeing on the terms of the deal, including the purchase price, payment terms, and other conditions. Integration entails bringing the two firms together, ensuring that processes are simplified, and workers are engaged and aligned with the new vision and objectives.

M&A is a sophisticated and multidimensional process that demands considerable study and strategy. It may be a successful approach for organizations trying to develop and extend their market share. But it may also be hazardous and expensive, and organizations must carefully consider the possible risks and advantages before starting on such deals. With effective strategy, execution, and integration, M&A can generate value and drive firm development in today's highly competitive business climate.

iv. Diversifying revenue streams.

Diversifying revenue streams is a business approach that includes earning money from many sources rather than depending on a single product, service, or client base. It is a crucial method for firms that wish to develop and survive in today's highly competitive industry. Given the changing business climate, a company's success depends on its capacity to adapt to changes in the economy and customer behavior. Consequently, diversifying income sources may allow firms to manage risk, boost profitability, and achieve long-term sustainability.

One of the advantages of diversifying income sources is that it may help organizations lessen their dependency on a particular product or service. Depending on a single product or service might be dangerous, as market trends and client preferences can change rapidly. Hence, firms that diversify their income sources may avoid placing all their eggs in one basket and decrease their exposure to market risks.

Diversifying income sources may also help firms boost their profitability. When a corporation has numerous sources of income, it may exploit each source to optimize revenue. For example, a firm that offers both goods and services may cross-sell to its current clients, boosting the entire value of each transaction. Moreover, organizations may utilize their current infrastructure to produce new income streams, such as renting out idle office space or selling surplus merchandise.

Additionally, diversifying income sources might help firms attain long-term viability. With many streams of revenue, firms are better positioned to withstand economic downturns or changes in client behavior. For example, a firm that depends significantly on a particular product may suffer if that product becomes outmoded. Yet, if the organization has diversified its income sources, it may pivot to other goods or services that are in demand.

To diversify income sources, firms should find new prospects for development and build a strategy to capitalize on them. This might entail expanding into new markets, generating new goods or services, or utilizing current assets in new ways. For example, a firm that offers software services may grow into consulting or training services. Conversely, a retail shop may offer things online to reach a larger client base.

Diversifying income sources is a vital strategy for firms that wish to develop and survive in today's competitive market. It may help firms decrease risk, boost profitability, and achieve long-term sustainability. By finding new prospects for development and devising a strategy to capitalize on them, organizations may generate a diverse income stream that is sustainable and lucrative.

www.ingramcontent.com/pod-product-compliance
Lightning Source LLC
Chambersburg PA
CBHW071139220526
45467CB00015B/1517